Kingdom of Diagonals

INDIANA UNIVERSITY POETRY SERIES

EDITOR: SAMUEL YELLEN

Kingdom of DIAGONALS

a book of poems 🦢 by Kenneth Slade Alling

Bloomington · INDIANA UNIVERSITY PRESS · 1954

"Gulls on a Rowboat" (1929); "Gull" (1931); "Hummingbird" (1932); "Clocks," "Water Snake," "Portrait of a Toad," "Cemetery Brook," and "Noon" (1933); "Dark Song" (1934); "Within Be Fed" and "Mown Hay" (1937); "Room," "Portrait," and "Iron Urn" (1939); "Wooden Statue," "Pumpkins," "Clock," and "Visitor" (1940); "Briareus" (1941); "Old Leaves," "Ploughed Field," "Turtle," and "'A Sun Dyall in a Grave'" (1943); "Autumn out of Summer," "Winter Frost," "Music," "Skeleton," "Identification," and "Old Man" (1944); "Batdom," "Woodpecker," "Yellow Bird," "Killdeer," "Moth," "Crow," and "Locusts, Etc." (1945); "Amazing Minute" and "Car Top" (1947); "Jack-in-the-Pulpit" and "Dead Wasp" (1948); "First World War," "Onion Skin in Barn," and "Dr. Donne" (1949); "Letter," "On the Park Bench," "Mind," "Pariah," and "Monsoon" (1950); and "The Toad," "Doves," "Oak," and "Quatrain" (1954), copyrighted in the respective years shown by *Poetry*.

LIBRARY OF CONGRESS CATALOG CARD NUMBER: 54-7971

MANUFACTURED IN THE UNITED STATES OF AMERICA

for E. W. A.

Acknowledgment

Grateful acknowledgment is made to the editors of *Poetry* for permission to use the poems in this book.

Contents

Kingdom of Diagonals

Gulls on a Rowboat

On the moored rowboat's gunwale perched,
As motionless as morning there,
Were seven gulls whose silence searched
The silent air.

Oddly I saw them so rescind
Their purposes, here side by side;
For gulls were made to wed the wind
And boats to marry with the tide.

Gull

The broken sea is but
A comb to comb his breast,
Who takes, with gull wings shut,
Tumultuously his rest,
Riding the height or hollow—
His body born to be
A subtle fire to follow
The great flame of the sea.

Hummingbird

You swallow, like a drawn bow driven,
And phoebe, always everywhere,
And to what else the sky is given,
Whatever walks with wings on air—
O birds, to whom all heaven's gateless,
You suddenly seem barred with bars:—
And heavy weights beside this weightless
Haunter of honey-chambered stars.

Clocks

This immemorial clock,
Whose dial is the girth
Of sea and hill and rock,
Entireties of earth,
Sounds with the falling sound
Of silver waters dropping,
So rhythmically bound,
Unaltered and unstopping.

And as those waters brim
The clock of earth and fall,
So round the solar rim
Fall the bright planets all,
Within that clock the sun:
Yet larger clocks than these
Await oblivion—
Altair; the Pleiades.

Water Snake

What ancient enmity between
Your race and mine could blind me to
The beauty of your flight in water!
Below the crying silver of
The brook-fall, like another brook,
With what consummate ease you flow!
Why must I shudder as I look?

Portrait of a Toad

With his heart beating in his throat,
With gold and onyx for his eyes,
His nostrils quivering to note
The far approach of flies,

The lichened toad lives in the meadow—
A waiter under apple trees;
A form, a shape, a naked shadow
Watching on bended knees.

Cemetery Brook

A river rounds this acre
And quietly divides
The sleeper and the waker.
The moon will touch its tides
Only with light, requiring
No such obeisance as
The sea must make. The tiring
Here in the summer grass
On this bank doze and dream;
And there the rested slumber
On that side of the stream—
And they are more in number.

Noon

Sun at the meridian
Leans too heavily on man,
Who requires a crutch of shade
Out of any good bough made;
And with this he is content
To support the firmament.

Dark Song

There must be green turf cut
Before graves can be made.
Give me a sharp spade; shut
The doors of light; the shade
Apparels best this labor:
Contrast were else too quick
Between our living neighbor,
Death's darkness, and those sick
With life's profound disorder,
Ephemerality.
I stand upon the border;
Give the bright steel to me.

Within Be Fed

Protect that darkness that
Indigenous to the soul,
In olden hours begat
Religion; art; the whole
Of permanence: the other
That throve in light is lost.
O ancient, elder mother,
Soul's darkness, we are tossed
Naked into the sun
With the ephemerae.
Defeat oblivion
For us, that else must die.

Mown Hay

The mown hay lies like moonlight on
This meadow in the summer sun.
The eye is hesitant to see,
With noon, night's luminosity
Rivering these fields: only the mind,
Friendly to phantoms, is resigned.

Room

Have you a room in common with the gods?
The wainscot darkness and the ceiling death;
With Cerberus and Sirius, the dogs
Of firmaments above and worlds beneath,
To fortify the old prodigious portal.
If you have not then you are not immortal.

Time shudders passing by that bitter door:
Catching the smell of permanence and frightened,
He listens for what feet are on that floor
And hearing, darts away, his horror heightened,
And hunting him and haunting him long after
The wind writhes like a sea with goatish laughter.

Portrait

His face a lichened rock:
His body a branching bole;
Where eighty Aprils nest
Like thrush or oriole.

His roots profound and free,
Rivered in hill and meadow:
But few men you will see
Palpable as his shadow.

Iron Urn

The toad has made himself a dusty couch,
To watch the urn's edge where two dragons crouch.
The paint's sun-bitten on this iron urn
Within the garden where the iris burn.
The toad has seen three generations walk
These garden paths but undisturbed they stalk
Each the coigned other on the crackled rim.
One dragon glares; the second glares at him:
Time-netted in this reticule of paint:
Their anger waxing with their souls' restraint.

Wooden Statue

(SPIRIT OF AUTUMN)

The sullen, seamless heaven's best
As frame and haven for these hues:
For this anomaly of gold,
The drowned leaf in the garden pool.

Old frosts have hacked their signatures
Into the oaken goddess, niched
Above the water with her child
Held close against the sapless heart.

She should be bronze: the water is:
The world is bronze: the patina
Of bronze is on the autumn trees;
Beneath the heavy, shineless heaven.

Pumpkins

Go, send a dragon. The Hesperides,
In bumper seasons, grew no fruit like these
Great gourds of gold; these apples that the ground,
That bendless bough, has grown. The old man found
Them hanging there. Go, send a dragon straight,
To guard the shed floor gorgeous with their weight.

Clock

The clock gnaws noisily the bone
Of time. With teeth like rat's or weasel's
The metal rodent chisels
A sustenance from stone.

Visitor

Come in. Familiar. Well, your features are.
The firm white scaffold underneath the face,
Viewed through the skin as green as some dead star;
Which won't clash with the color in this place;
Your father and your mother knit together
Neatly in passionate, prehistoric weather.

Come in. Come in. I knew that you would come.
In every room the phosphorus is lit.
You needn't feel your way about my home.
The rooms; the rooms; the rooms are infinite.
We'll visit some new room, my clacking friend,
This time, down corridors that have no end.

Briareus

Hold out the thicket of your hands
Where I can run at last and hide;
Briareus, immerse me in
The ragged waters of your side.

The Titans with their terror march;
The Titans like a massive sea.
Reach out your fingered rivers now,
Briareus, unbroken tree.

Old Leaves

Old leaves, the angled dust, are in my hand
And if I close and crush the weightless planes
I'll lose the palpability that now
Pleases the flesh which loves that strange embrace.
What is it that the flesh loves in these forms,
Hard but not heavy, edged but not like knives?

Ploughed Field

The steel prow of the farmer's ship
Rides in the farmer's sea.
The great waves rise; the great waves lip
The iron and curl away.

The farmer from the bridge commands
The furrowed ocean; steers
His vessel toward the promised land
And fruitage of the years.

Turtle

Contemporaneous with the angels' fall,
The carapace, a curved, Byzantine wall,
Pointed with gold like some mosaicked niche,
Stands in the dark museum of the ditch.

"A Sun Dyall in a Grave"

DONNE

By this, some pour of darkness might be stayed
And bleed beside the sunless blade,
Severed, a shadow darker even than
Its element subterranean,
To write
For those dead eyes the time of night.

Autumn out of Summer

In the sultry August weather yesterday
I heard the first nut strike the barn roof, knew
The infallible hickory would fetch with this,
As in all years that I remember, autumn,
But had forgot his full art, how he could
Invoke in one night autumn out of summer,
Until I saw the morning hyaline
And the trees furbished, felt the blade of air,
Its edge restored, now good for cutting with.

Winter Frost

The silver ferns unfold their fronds.
There is no copper in the bronze
With which the garden hill's embossed.
In this white jungle of the frost,
This metal forest, you can see
Precisions of the sudden tree,
Whose seed sown in the earth of air,
Found April and found August there
Without duration. Winter's loins
And incandescent ardor joins
Conception, birth, maturity,
In the same instant in this tree;
As if from spring in one green stroke
Burst acorn and the centuried oak.

Music

Exhale your vapor, fallen snow,
And fashion from your breath the fog;
Ceiling me in with cry of crow
And the dim bay of dog.

Those lonely syllables have been
Rich music in this room before,
Mingled, immured with me between
White wall and weightless door.

Skeleton

The feathered hill of early morning
Becomes with light a place of trees;
The spare personae of that myth
Of winter summer never sees.

I look and avid too for edge
Undulled, unblurred by appetite,
Put off the flesh and on that ledge,
Among them stand bone-bright.

Identification

He sees himself innumerably repeated;
His replicas in that prodigious glass,
Whereof the wall that fronts him is a frame;
Or the unmargined mirror multiplying
His entity, his lineaments, his face,
A thousand fold, ten thousand thousand times;
As if his self were a seed that had burst
Into a sudden banyan everywhere.

Old Man

With evening he puts off concealment, not
So much the hidden as the far withheld,
And when we lift our eyes from work we spot
The movement of a larger mouse the belled
Mind watches; wonders;—and the thing is caught.

No one has heard his foot upon the stair,
Or if the foot was noiseless, seen the form.
Behind that packing case some door of air
Is opened and he enters as if from
A silence silently into the room.

Batdom

The swallow, by the evening light
Transmuted, puts on batdom, flies,
Bedemonizing with his antics
The darkening skies.

The edge, the bright periphery
Of wing, the grace in morning air,
The night's obliquely bent to that
Refraction there.

Woodpecker

The pastel shades in sky, on hill,
His pastel breast, that bird's, repeats,
As with his opulent design
He walks December's naked streets.
Like one who visits house to house
He goes about the winter boughs.

Come spring; come summer; autumn, come,
Progenitors of this and see
The waxing grandeur of this room;
Perceive yourselves' maturity;
Stand here beside me now and view
The year itself, divest of you.

Yellow Bird

Come build in this bush, yellow bird.
O, summer warbler, weave your home,
Corniced in these curved pillars. Nest
Your brood in the bright room.

With golden petals, golden sun,
With golden feathers undertake
To hood the eyes of memory
Where crawls the climbing snake.

Killdeer

The green blur of invading foliage
Precluded edge, precluded line,
And looking out, I must acknowledge,
I said, the pattern is not mine,
And I must wait for winter scarp
And winter bough for something sharp
And permanent in its design.

When on the ground prepared before me,
And graded and regrassed there stood
The visitation to restore me.
Incised upon the summer wood,
I watched it walk, that black and white bird,
And praised the god that sent the right bird
To break me from my barren mood.

Moth

The saffron moth,
The antlered thing,
With pale gold fur
And patterned wing,
In silence sings the song
It is not given bird to sing.

Crow

Indelible of breast and wing,
He is a period between
The sentences of winter and
The broken syntax of the spring.

He punctuates the seasons, these
With postures; sitting, comma, colon,
And flying far about the swollen
Summer a clear parenthesis.

Locusts, etc.

The metal birds that agitate
Some wire of wind within their throats,
Strum on the iron filament,
Their arid notes;

Sit as the orchestra of drouth,
Tiered in the tired branches, play
The symphony that was composed
For the last day.

Amazing Minute

The house has the cohesion of the stairs;
The stairs cohere in him, in his ascent,
Who traverses that brief plateau, the landing.—
In this amazing minute all who mount
Their million terraces of stone or wood
And all their purposes are soluble
In his identity, what each ascends for,
The open book forgotten on the table,
Sleep, petty thieving, fornication, murder,
Whatever mission's possible in him.
The house contains this elaborate container.
All climbs with him these treads that his feet climb.

Car Top

I clean the car top and gaze down
At tree leaves strataed in strange water.
Unorbited as butterflies
The replicas above them flutter.

But in this pond, by what illusion
That says the element's less arid,
Some law precludes their like confusion.
The movement's weightier that's mirrored.

Dead Wasp

The small wasp lies in state,
A formidable design in black and gold:
Tiered like a Chinese tower, his abdomen;
His wings as hyaline as heaven,
Windows the now elegiac light pours through.

Jack-in-the-Pulpit

Beside the stone work on the north side where
The sun's excluded always, blooms this flower.

It feeds on darkness as the rose on light;
Shade is its wafer, shadow its rich meat.

First World War

After the Armistice I was at Tours,
Where the girls grew on trees
And where the shaking of any bough would shower
You with dozens of these.

Were the gods good? In their ironic way.
Hyderabad's Nizam would,
Ancestrally schooled in the zenana, say
The gods were good.

Brought up by generations (as was I)
That came to a bleak coast,
And always under the surveillance of my
Grandfather's ghost,

I found the harem alien, troublesome,
And having it in haste,
Unmanageable. I was overcome
By the sudden East.

Onion Skin in Barn

It looks a piece of golden, broken glass,
This fragment here of what entire it was:—
From a Venetian furnace long ago,
To set with strange light some king's room aglow.
But fallen on this drab and dusty floor
It has its palace as it had before.

Dr. Donne

The grave came to him, at his wish, before
He could come to the grave and when he died
He did return the visit, nothing more;
The social debt to death was satisfied.

Letter

"It's just because I'm back in a dreary place."
Your dreariness spoken makes my dreariness less.
You are a siphon for my dreariness.
Time that effaces much for us won't efface,
My correspondent, this anomaly;—
And not because I'm man and you are woman,
But as we are intolerably human,
That mine is soluble in your agony.

On the Park Bench

On the park bench the man, alone,
Playing chess, "a game of pure skill."
He walks in a kingdom of diagonals
The moon's gravity orders his steps
The traffic is all of his own making but
If he runs himself down
He won't die
He'll only be deported.

Mind

The old panes distort the trees,
Lift some bough jaggedly.
Mind, flow awry like the glass;
Refract the sentence you say;
Fever the syntax.

You have in sleep,
Umbilical to nightmare,
Gone on like this;
When Saturn weighed your paragraphs
And everything with shudder danced.

Pariah

The continent cried out of a dog's mouth
An early morning dog struck down in the street
Outside a whore's window
The whore and her buyer
The dog was their bastard
Conceived at midnight
Born after a gestation of ninety minutes
Matured in another ninety
And dying
Crying out to his parents and the world—
And the peninsula and all struck-down dogs
Howling out of his mouth.

Monsoon

Walk in the half light of rain
Backwards
Into the rain
Of a rainy city.
It wasn't the destination
The terminal
You fevered for then,
It was the ride in the *gharri*
The smell of the bazaar
That stays with you;
It wasn't the girl,
It was the old horse
And the *gharri-wallah*
That your annas took.
Your annas bought more it seems than your rupees did
In lasting pleasure.
The rain came to the city in a *gharri* too,
That *gharri-wallah* kept his fare waiting.
You were the rain that wanted your city
City in city
The great city only the environs
Of your small intricate city
And the *gharri* so slow in getting you there.

The Toad

His silence inside him
His language on his back
An idol of awe in the garden
The toad
His orbs older than Jupiter.

Doves

The doves get up;
The field flings them:
Out of the flock I am parcelled three to watch,
Each making of the horizontal air
His cliff to pitch from;
But if the air *was* palpable,
It would splinter with the force of their going;
As rock would splinter,
Intercepting the velocity of these hollow bones.

Oak

The oak talks in winter
The leaf's edge transmuted into the word's edge
The wind knows the syntax of the tree
The crescendos
The silences
The bookless language
The pageless speech.

Quatrain

The bleak fields antlered with the fallen branches,
The young men leave; goodby to the boughed fields;
The stones urge them elsewhere; longing is lost here;
What's in it for them; the cold yes of the rocky scarp.